Out of Place

Out of Place

Poems

Richard Jackson

THE ASHLAND POETRY PRESS

Printed in the United States of America

ISBN: 978-0-912592-77-0

Library of Congress Control Number: 2013955814

Cover art: Metka Krasovec, "Waiting for Spring in Tompkins Park," acrylic oil on canvas, 129 x 160 cm.

Cover design: Nicholas Fedorchak

Author photo: Terri Harvey

Acknowledgements

American Literary Review, "No End to It," "Prophecy"
Asheville Poetry Review, "While You Were Away," "Visionary"
Atlanta Review, "The Terezin Ghetto"
Blackbird, "Walking the Dog," "Prayer"
BODY Literature, "Revision," "Tip of My Tongue"
Borderlands, "Out of Place"
Brilliant Corners, "Bosnian Elegy," "Negative Capability," "Signs and Wonders," "What Comes Next," "Traffic Jam"
Cerise Press (Paris), "Another Small Apocalypse"
Chattahoochee Review, "The Rest," "Jacob's Fear"
Cortland Review, "Letter from Tuscany," "Letter from Slovenia"
Crab Orchard Review, "The Storm," "My Many Disguises"
Crazyhorse, "Sifting"
Cutthroat, "Abraham's Journey," "Is This the Person to Whom I Am Speaking," "Where the World Comes to Me"
Georgia Review, "About This Poem," "At the Confederate Graveyard, Chattanooga," "The Secret," "Everything All at Once"
Grist, "Otherness," "Facebook," "Misunderstood"
Massachusetts Review, "Living On"
Miramar, "Sarsaparilla"
Redivider, "Isaac's Consent"
Salon@615, "Letter from Slovenia," "Letter from Tuscany"
Smartish Pace, "Not Here, Not There" "Preemptive Elegy," "The Ethical Problem of Existence"
Southern Indiana Review, "Belief," "Endurance"
Upstreet, "Certainty"

"Sarsaparilla" first appeared in *First Light: A Festschrift for Philip Levine.*

"Endurance" appeared in *Verse Daily.*

"While You Were Away," "Visionary," and "Signs and Wonders" also appeared in *Southern Poetry Anthology VI.*

for Terri,
and for Amy, Anna, Emily, and Daryl

Contents

III

*The dead and the living, those that awake and those
sleeping, the young and the old, are one and the
same in us; the one, moved from its place is the other,
and the other returned to its place is the one.*

　　　　　　　　　　　　　　　　　　— Heraclitus

*Even though the house is quiet and shut,
Even though I am not in it, I am in it.*

　　　　　　　　　　　　　　— Juan Ramón Jiménez

*My shadow and the shadow of the snail are one and
the same.*

　　　　　　　　　　　　　　　　— James Wright

*The earth is moved from its position by the weight of
a little bird upon it.*

　　　　　　　　　　　　　— Leonardo, Notebooks

I

You are like a cloud
Glimpsed between the branches. In your eyes there shines
The strangeness of a sky that isn't yours.

— *Cesare Pavese*

Another life, of the city at nightfall. Another soul, of one
who watches the night.

— *Pessoa*

And if I... understand all mysteries and all knowledge,
and if I have all faith, so as to remove mountains,
but do not have love, I am nothing.

— *1 Cor. 13:2*

About This Poem

At the beginning... which is to awaken you to the right kind of Joy
in serious times, we must list all those who have been killed
since I last wrote... .
— *Bonhoeffer, 1942, Germany*

It has to account for its untied shoelaces as well as its Extermination
Camps. Sitting among all those languages in the Munich beer garden.
Hitler's first speech a few blocks away. A masked ball where
the costumes are all switched around. Those carnival grab bags
filled with joy or remorse. Above me the clouds are paralyzed.
I have to wipe the dust from my soul. The wind holds its breath.
Bosnia, 1994: one group of men forced to bite off the testicles
of another group. Others to stand in the snow till their feet rot.
These things orbit now like a planet too far to see. Even the bee
can't figure a way out of my stein. Light staggers through the trees.
Every moment is filled with other moments. According to Bell's
Theorem whatever happens to this bee influences a history yet
to be written. Like the seed stars that smudge the trail of Mira as
it slips across the sky. All my maps are smudged with atrocities.
There are so many voices that are our own voices. Rhythm is just this
oscilloscope of the soul. We come from a place that has always
been inside us. Our words migrate helplessly. The world reflects
only itself. Which is why we have to create our own memories.
The paths from here spread out like shattered glass. The man
across the table's from Krakow. He doesn't want to talk about
the occupation and its lives turned to smoke. Only the mechanical
Trumpeter in his church spire. The song stops where his real
ancestor was felled by an enemy's arrow. In the silence that follows
don't we all have to begin again? At the end of a line, the door
left open for a moment where you can fall in love, remember
what you wanted to forget, forget what you wanted to remember.

Why do we think our metaphors will save us? The world is only
itself. Time is just our way of imagining it. At least the bee has
ultraviolet vision to see everything we can't. We have to light
our dark spaces with the sputtering matches of our words.
We have to follow wherever they lead us. There's this little
hole in existence we all pass through. Someone is always entering.
He's the one who invents me while I think I am writing about him.

Traffic Jam

for Tomas and Monica

Like one of those feelings you can't get rid of,
there's a crack in the windshield from road debris and
I'm listening to Coleman Hawkins' great solo, *Picasso*,
but the word is that an eighteen wheeler has blown across
the median at mile marker 296 and we are at 312, barely
moving, and he's taken out another truck, at least three dead,
the guy at the Conoco said, offering a different route
which we ignore for our own curiosity to see death up close,
but those three people, what dreams did they forget
to dream, what dreams did they leave back at the front door,
no end to them, the birds trying to speak for them,
the buds of new light trying not to wilt, the words they
say to each other going mute,

                    because the most horrific moment
comes only once as Schopenhauer said, but it is not yet here,
which is why we project our futures into the rear view and
why all I have now to hope with is Hawkins' changing tempo,
these branches dipping one way then another in the wind, and him
filling the music with mystery, intensifying everything,

and as long as he does that I can believe the story isn't true,
the nest of cloud has not begun to trap the light, the roadside
trees stand their ground against the wind that could blow
any of us off course, as long as I can't imagine what
it would be like to have that truck heading for me though
all I can see ahead of me now is a line of red lights popping
on and off like those interactive maps that trace a battle line
or hiking path, no end to it, though the truck in the next lane from

South Dakota probably sees more, ahead of him is Oklahoma,
we're all over the map here,

and that's the problem, isn't it,
this trying to get beyond ourselves, trying to get beyond
what William of Ockham (1285-1347) meant when he said
the only real words describe simple objects and not feelings
which is why it is so hard to say things like love and hope
and regret, although I am thinking here of Tomas and Monica
talking without words that day in 1996, Lake Bled,
the war all around us still, no end to the tortures and executions,
but also how those two souls could make the morning into
a kind of prayer by nods and gestures, by pointing
and by tracing figures in the dust,

how we have to invent ourselves
each time we speak because everything we say has been
a secret even to ourselves, no end to it, and when we discover it
we don't know how to capture it except by pointing so that
we have to see words as if they were things after all, and the fear is
that I might see exactly what happened up the road,

because
as Leibnitz (1646-1716) showed, we are always trying
to connect names and times to ourselves, as he did
mapping everything he knew into one linked system
in an age when some of the maps were in the shape of hearts,
cartography, they called it, as a way to follow your own
conscience in getting from here to what Robert Vivian calls
the "Land of Benediction" not this river of traffic, even if it upset

church and state leading to all that violence, all that dying,
no end to it, not just those people up the road, and not just
the ten girls blown up in Afghanistan fetching water
who rest now beneath the sadness of a few broken trees
or the other deaths the wind has blown in from India
and Connecticut, from the burnt branches, all that's left
from a few villages in the Congo, all of this coursing like
the endless shadows of coyotes I fear are blinking along
the deep eddies of the tree line,

                      and there he goes again,
Hawkins, just when I am ready to despair, sounding
like shadows that seem to waver in the wind when
there is no wind

            —but why *Picasso* except that every story can be
broken into whatever we want to see or hear to be the truth,
what Sextus Empiricus said 1800 years ago, which is why there is
no end to the way we seek and hate these stories where the gun
or bomb or accident has made its horrible, untranslatable gesture,

but I think Hawkins had in mind Picasso's blue period,
that family of three on the beach unable to face each other
or what would happen next, and it's not, as J.S. Mill said,
that we need to fondle other people's deaths to imagine
our own, bitter as that is, like the asbestos smell of the truck
brakes in the December air, where the birds are becoming
other seasons

           and it's true I have driven despair into my life
for too long now, what with all these names and ideas lining up,

trying to chart, through them, some meaning for all this violence,
as long as our words don't replace our losses, those souls
we make into our own, but only create a kind of present tense just as
one hawk traces the wavering eddies in the air above us
and the other Hawk lets the hope in his lungs breathe life
into the car each time I hit replay, as long as the marsh
off to the right shimmers like tinfoil and the trees speak
their language of gestures and tracings, as long as his breath,
which is also this mysterious wind, gathers all these tones into
a time I can find no single word or map for—other than love,
other than this music which I'll call, dear souls, my prayer.

Sarsaparilla

for Phil Levine

I'll never know what words my Uncle Bernard chose
to connect the Belgian landscape with his B-17 as it
pancaked down after helping his crew bail out. *Sarsaparilla*,
my father says, because he and Bernard used it to mean
Surprise and *there's nothing left to do*, but that was 1954
and we were making Sarsaparilla, a kind of intense rootbeer,
to store it in those dark green used bottles in the closet.
I believed that if the wrong word seeped in the bottles
would explode. Bernard went down as Bonhoeffer was
looking for words to argue against Hitler. Spain was
already lost. I would learn later that is was not history
but space that mattered.

You can see dusk expand now
across the pond's surface. The wind gets tangled
in the trees. Words disappear into the woods, trails
into forgotten ravines. It's as if each word enclosed
a secret meaning impossible to guess, or the voices
we thought we buried still echoed like the bells
they used to place above graves in case the dead had
something to say.

I think that's what Hardy meant
when he had his corpses listen to gunnery practice
instead of the apocalypse. My father knew how all wars
just try to find another word for space. I remember him
telling the story of Joseph yelling from the bottom of a well
while his brothers claimed his land. Today a few
words crash through a Sinai border crossing,

a few others build a town on someone else's land,
another scatters its meanings across a temple
whose words it cannot understand.

                                 Here, a few
stars call out. A few late birds scour for crumbs.
There are languages no one understands. There are
three new stars from the Milky Way each year
that have no name. That's ten million since
our first ancestors walked on earth. *Sarsaparilla!*
my father would have whistled. I don't know
a better reason to keep looking for words that rise
beyond us like the red *sprites* that light the edge
of space and send their secret messages into
the furthest corners of the universe.

                                 Tonight
shapes start to speak from the pond's surface under
the borrowed light of the moon. When one of
my father's bottles burst the others echoed it
filling the room with the sweet smell of failure.

Joseph, from the bottom of a well, could see,
even at noon, day stars he had thought were invisible.
Sarsaparilla he too would have cried in hope if he knew
the word. There is one star which is the bottle galaxy,
edging towards a Black Hole, but spraying its words out,
as my father knew, with its countless and relentless stars
that mean the love that connects us over time which is
space, which is all the love we have, or could ever have.

Bosnian Elegy

The tops of trees still clutch, fiercely, the last light.
There's a bird caught in the chimney. Its complaint
trembles down the empty corridors of the heart.
The moon struggles to define itself behind a few thin
masks of cloud.
                    I remember the Sax player in Sarajevo
playing *Solitude* as if Coleman Hawkins fingered
the keys as he did on that old recording my father
kept, each layer of harmony rubbing against the wall
and slipping through the alley to where, later, the market
would be bombed.
                    Why can't I get that song out of my head?
How much space does any memory take up? After
a while our pasts become abandoned buildings, or like
the sudden supernova whose light appeared for a few days
before moving through space to another galaxy.
                                                There's
always another mass grave to discover. The crickets begin
to panic. For a while our memories fall into the crevices
of the mind. Our words imitate our losses.
                                        For a while
we too can forget the love we didn't show or the people
we have hurt.
                    We become the empty spaces in our dreams.
Tonight, a few invisible stars still keep their distance.
I can hear the leaves fall through the darkness.
                                            In Hell,
Aeneas grabbed the empty air he thought was his father.
Plato thought the real took up no space at all. All these

memories seem out of tune. Hawkins' solitude was all
that he could bear.

                In a while that chimney bird stops but sound
keeps coming. There's always an invisible wind that rips
at the stars. Sometimes I think there is an invisible *other*
who occupies every mirror.

                              My friend says she avoids
trouble by becoming invisible. My voice distrusts my ear.
There's always a few memories to scar the air. There's
no secret that is secret. Our hopes are only grace notes.

There's always that image I can't push aside, the family outside
Banja Luka, in the charred cellar, the man's fist raised above
the other bodies, melded in defiance where they were
burnt alive.

                Tonight the hissing of stars is more than I can bear.

Otherness

It is part of our disguise that our dreams are lived by someone else.
Thales dreamt an eclipse in 570 BC and stopped a war. You arrived
subconsciously in a sentence I was reading from a book I never
finished. What we say gets its meaning from what we don't say.
Persephone kept her love hidden underground. So much of what
we feel is habit. We need to search for a way to say what is real:
the air filled with the simple pungency of cut grass, the flowers
barely breathing, the black and azure butterflies mating in clusters
by the side of the trail, the melancholy taste of blackberries
some bear had abandoned at my approach, the stag that lifts
its head unconcerned, whatever drifts away, whatever stays.
How do we keep our own dreams from touching each other?
I remember, as a boy, fearing for the snail as it crawled out
from its shell, I imagined for love. I couldn't coax it back.
What we do is a metaphor for what we don't do. These are
the only ways to tell you what I mean. In Chagall's drawings
the faces of his lovers are surprised by their own sadness that
they have not become one of his angels smudged across the sky.
Their nights disguise themselves among the noontime shadows.
At the tomb, Mary Magdalene thought Jesus was a gardener.
What we know gets its meaning from what we don't know.
It is why we create stories for those Mayan cities still buried
beneath the jungles of Mexico. Everything is a metaphor.
Those butterflies on the trail, for instance, I thought
they carried part of the sky on their wings. Or the cloud
rising like a ruined column from some ancient site supporting
the sky's idea of it. In a while the wind convinces it to collapse
as it does with so many of our dreams. What we dream
gets its meaning from what we don't dream. Memory betrays us:
The sentence I read as you appeared was a piece of smooth

ocean glass where Nicholas of Cusa dreamt of spiritual beings
living near the sun. Anaximander knew we emerged from
sea creatures. What if you had appeared with those few snowy
egrets this morning who seemed puzzled or fearful at my presence?
What we love gets its meaning from what we don't love.
The air here seems filled with fragments of some other day.
In a drawing I saw once, my words shivered for how the stag
gazed tenderly at the wolves, as if to say they had no other choice,
as if to forgive them as they ate so ravenously from its side.
No, never again have I dreamt such a perfect love.

While You Were Away

for Terri

Sleeves of sunset hung empty over the brown hills.
Ice from the North Pole kept floating this way. Locusts
sprouted like seedlings. I was floating under the ice
in my dream, but you never saw me. The windows were
boarded up. Later the clouds argued, then left in a huff.
There's a hidden tax in everything we say. I meant
for this poem to glow in the dark like one of those
old statues of saints my father kept on the dashboard
to guide the way.

But aren't we always lost? Desire
punches a time clock that always reads the same hour.
There's a suspicion that today is really yesterday.
That crickets dream about being reincarnated as pure
sound. The bees wake as the sun hits the hive.
The sky is filled with late and clumsy birds.
Somebody's always ready to pickpocket the past.
There's a gap in the narrative the way a river
suddenly slips underground but flows on unnoticed.
Now they think the vegetative state has some neuron
activity. I worry that most of my own memories are
water soluble. There are places inside me so remote
the inhabitants never see each other. The worm never
sees the robin. Whitetip reef sharks catch a prey
by sensing the electric impulses in its muscles. Auto
cannibalism occurs when the Hutu militia of east Congo
make their captives eat their own flesh. Feel free to add
whatever you want there, but it won't make it any better.

Every war is reincarnated as another war. Even Paul
retreated to a cave in the Tarsus foothills when things
went bad. He preached about love but nobody has
ever really withstood its test. Some of his flock never
returned. *A species stands beyond*, wrote Dickinson.
Almost every species of small bird comes to my feeder.
Maybe everything is a test. Like how I am going to get you
back into this poem. *I'll git you in my dreams,* Leadbelly
sang to Irene. This was going to be a Valentine poem
because today is Valentine's Day, which replaced Lupercalia,
the Roman fertility feast, but that was before the daily news
broke in. And before tomorrow had already forgotten us.

The great love poet, Leopardi, never knew a woman.
Modigliani loved every woman he met, and painted them
in order to leave them. Queen Nefertiti's eye makeup
stopped infections, but its lead base drove her mad.
She wanted to be born again as the brightest star. She read
her future in the cloudy hatchery of the Milky Way.
If space weren't a vacuum we couldn't bear its decibel level.
The Hutu slaughter women who learn to read, then joke that
it's a form of reincarnation. They think they live on
the dark side of the moon. The sky is gnarled with clouds.
There's a low fog covering another war in the foothills.
The stars are no longer the gods we took them for.
The moon is a turtle that needs to right itself.

I don't really know how to tell you all this. It's as if
I were left at the doorway of one of your dreams.
If only these words wouldn't conspire against me.

But even Love is an unsolvable equation. Leadbelly
kept singing because his own song never worked except
in his dreams. I'm still floating in mine. I don't have
any Faith in a solution. You can't just turn off the news.
It's getting late—best to guess *None of the Above*.
All we have left is the astronomy of Hope. The hills have
their own geometry. Paul said we devour our own souls.
Maybe it's just the way the day grows up and leaves us.

It all comes down to the same thing in the end which is
what everything has been pointing to since the beginning.
When you're gone, you see, all these worries spin around
like those childhood tops that zigzag until they bump
into something that stops them, like this, for example,
another simple mention of you, if only for later reference.

Signs and Wonders

The morning avoids us. The streets walk through town and
never look back. Trees whisper secrets and we think it is
just the wind. The echo of the moon is fading. There's a worn
saxophone in the corner filled with unplayed notes. The pigeons
on the walk nod their heads and mumble to its music. The water
a cactus holds is the desert music Williams so loved. The foreign
planet that has wandered into our own galaxy, origin unknown,
has a plan for us it won't reveal. And why should it? The soot
we leave on Tibetan glaciers melts them. Diseases creep
towards the warmer north. Someone invades a home or
a country and it hardly wakes an image. A child is torn by
an abuser and no one reports it. The man selling pretzels,
the man sleeping under the cardboard on the bench,
each one has his own shoebox of memories. Our own shoes
are filling with borders. The bonfires of our souls fall in on
themselves. It's as if we must tune our silences to a lost key.

Love? How do we give ourselves to another and not lose
our selves? We have to learn how even the objects around us
hide their pain. We can't listen to the heart's ventriloquists.
It's a fact that music raises our endorphin levels which kills pain.
Ben Webster *In the Wee Small Hours of the Morning* would
let his tremulous breath slide emotionally beneath his
saxophone's sensuous fingering, but was called *Brute* for the pain
he'd inflict, later, in a bar. My father, listening to Gene Krupa's
wild drum, would say the emptiness behind each note is just
the ghost of what we could do to each other. How lucky we are,
he'd say, not to calculate the decay of our own sun. The light hides
now behind skirts of rain. When scientists let hydrogen antimatter
collide with matter we delight in its pure energy and try

to ignore the destruction that always follows. These are all
the signs I know. They point to a world behind this one. Webster's
bulging eyes would tell us there is always more. The tracks of
the past outdistance our dreams of it. And what was he gesturing
towards, years later, my father, his mind nearly porous, seeing those
three frightened pigeons, if not the pure, inescapable flight of his heart?

Visionary

I could feel a few dying stars hovering over my shoulder
but that wasn't it. Not the fact that there are so few
sunspots anymore, and therefore fewer Northern Lights.
Not the problem of the thinning arctic ice. And yet weren't they
all connected somehow? Weren't they symptoms of something
I couldn't see. How many people saw the naked man fleeing
Christ's betrayal in Gethsemene? Fish nibble at the moon's
reflection. Camels have two eyelids, one transparent,
so they can see in sandstorms. We see only what we want
to see, only a fraction of what this stone has seen in a few
billion years. Now the stone wants to be an apple. The night
splinters. The sky trembles piteously. The real world appears
in the reflection of the soldier's face on a green radar screen.

Maybe there are some things we are not supposed to see.
The town beneath the lake. The cells that will divide mercilessly
in a few decades. I have been looking at Chagall for whom
every object is transparent. He thought that some of his dreams
were dreamt in other people's minds. That's why his images
echo each other from distant points on the canvas. Everything
we see hides a world someone else sees. If you don't finish this
poem it won't exist. Neither will I. Where do we come from when
we come to ourselves? There's a common thread that hasn't
been established yet. Cendrars said that Chagall painted a church
with a church, a cow with a cow. He painted his own love, Bella,
floating up to kiss him. A hawk's flight unravels the thread we never
knew was there. There's a smell of smoke smudging through
the trees, but no fire.

These words migrate towards invisible
meanings. It would be hard to predict what follows.
Each hour seems ready to kidnap the next for ransom.
How many orphans blindly follow some warlord around
the streets of Mogadishu with an AK-47 and a sack of grenades?
This is not the symbol or allegory you might take it for.
Behind them, if you look carefully, there's a mother fleeing
her burning house with a wheelbarrow full of children.
She seems to gaze from the beginning of time. The day turns
into ash. The evening is exhausted. It lies like a shed snakeskin.

It is only slowly now that the poem gathers itself around
these unexpected events. In Chagall's *Poet Reclining*
the pastoral world behind him is both dreamt and real.
He seems to lie in front of, not in the picture. You can't see
who is in the building or in the woods. You have to look for
what is out of place. We need, like Blake, to look through
and not with the eye. The paths from here spread out like
cracks in ice. The skaters trace patterns you can only see
from above. How am I going to see my way clear of all this?
Everything I say brings its endless army of associations.
In another poem the mother would be pushing a shopping cart.
We can hope for another poem to emerge out of the shadows.
There's nothing we can do about the guns or the warlords.
It will have to show a way that looks like truth, but
it will have to show it through these broken windows.
You have to see it to believe it, but you'll never see it coming.

The Terezin Ghetto

It was hard to tell if you were still living. Shallows of hope
still hug the banks of the River Ohře where the ashes
of nearly 22,000 people were dumped in 1944. They must
still live somehow in the plants and drinking water
that returns to Prague. And the children's drawings,
the poems, the music written and performed here
stowed away in hidden crevices. Alena Steinmova's drawing
of a bunk and her family, and what's that?—an angel
floating through the bottom mattress, a protector
or someone gone to smoke. Even now the streets are empty.
Does one live here out of ignorance or duty? Only dozens
of cats, suspicious, shy. They are the angels Alena dreamt.
They seem to float here to fill the silences between
our words. The maple the children planted is still here.
The streets follow the same rigid pattern.
These are the walls they left their sweaty prayers on,
the streets they scuffed. The fields beyond that are yellow
with mustard. The wind that keeps molding the clouds
into the same shapes. What does the river think
as it approaches another river? All I can do is copy
down a few of the poems they left. Every word
like the inhabitant of Kafka's *Burrow* hearing all those
other words. Or the way Ovid, exiled near Constance
on the Black Sea, his ghetto, worried he was losing
his perfect Latin to the grunts of the barbarians. Celan knew
you have to redeem each barbaric language until
it breaks open its coffin but could never break open his own.
Every ghetto presses its boot heels into the soul.
Here the mass graves try to burrow deeper into the earth.
On the banks of Ovid's Danube the mounds of some prehistoric

people try to rise up from the Delta. As if there were
a difference. What did they think their lives would mean
to us? Time closes more doors than it opens. Words are
no better than scattered leaves. Our best thoughts are just
graffiti in a universe that speaks another language.
The immense sorrow of the sun as it slides down behind
the crematoria. The way stars whisper their coming deaths.
Maybe everything we write is written in the future.
It's the only way to keep on living. During the ghetto years
the only vehicle you could see here was a horse-drawn hearse.

Prayer

Kutná Hora Bone Church, Sedlec, CZ

History percolates in the face of the bewildered angel
holding a skull under one arm and blowing her apocalyptic
trumpet in the other. There are 40,000 sets of bones in
the shapes of chandeliers, columns, temples. I am thinking
of Jan Hus who used to practice being burned as a martyr,
and whose secret followers I imagine displayed here.
His bones are buried in the wind, his words spoken by
blind stars. None of the bones here remember what bodies
they belong to. It is a hard thing to realize that each of
the bones once loved as we do, and harder even to say it.
Vowels of wind brush across the windows. Hus's words
and the words of the ground fog are the same words.
Huge snails climb up the sides of the church. The walls
are cracked like old skin. My own words have frayed edges.
Still, I can place you here in one sentence that tries to forget
all this death. There's a mesh of pine trees trying to capture
some stray light. Here and there a prayer emerges between
inexplicable phrases. None of the bones are listening.
None of the bones remember the hush of insects. With each
death a new day, but the crickets sound the same, the shadows
disappear like yesterday's shadows. These bones only wanted
to make a difference, not be a part of some grotesque figure.
Hus was burned for saying things not even these bones understand.
There's a leisurely rain beginning. It doesn't stop the tiny white
moths that have no idea of their own mortality. It doesn't stop
the frantic crows from reminding us of our own bones as they
pick at the body of a mole. The light is turning into cobwebs.
The day seems distracted. What memory has in store for us
we never know. There's a jar of earth here from Golgotha

some Abbot thought (1278) would make this ground sacred.
I am thinking of your own sacred garden. I am thinking of
your robins that rock on the telephone wires like men at prayer.
The air here is mottled with all these dreams. Above me
the swifts write a random history of the soul. Against them,
I put these words for you, a kind of prayer themselves,
a way to redeem the silences these bones announce, something
about the way we live our loves, forever on the verge of believing.

The Rest

Walter Butts, in memoriam

Restless sky. A moon leaning over like a prayer.
Its pond's reflection revealing more and more.
There's a nest waiting for a bird, or a leaf waiting
for a tree.

       Meanwhile you've stepped into your own
unexpected, unexplored world. The eyes adjust
to the darkness and see what no one else can see.

Anaxagoras thought the whole cosmos was a single
mind. There are a dozen white dwarfs surrounded
by graveyards of stars waiting in our own galaxy
to blindside us.

       Today they found two fingers and
a tooth stolen in the 18th century from Galileo's
tomb to put on display. They rest there like planets
or stars he forgot to catalogue. If only we could bribe
the clock.

       The wind is angry. Light jabs at the shadows.
The sparrow that took refuge on my screen porch can't
get out. Its idea is to turn itself into an angel.

       In 1789
Herschel described the heavens as the Garden of Eden.
It was, he knew, a world where the eye could never rest.

Now the sky has abandoned its clouds. Hardly anyone
I know believes in God.

Sometimes the rain freezes
so high up in the atmosphere it never touches earth,
but it is still raining above us. To have a belief
doesn't mean to have a reason. Mangrove leaves
collect salt and fall off, saving the rest of the tree.

Any consolation we have is the dream of another
consolation. A road waiting for a traveler.

Every death
drifts through the heart like cries from invisible
galaxies.

The stars have turned their backs on us. You've
left, now, simply because the sky has fallen asleep.

The Ethical Problem of Existence

What I thought was an ethical problem
of existence was only just a broken heart.
— Jack Myers

A night with stars inching across the sky like ticks.
The lost moon, or only a spotlight from a store opening.
A mind without the wings it so desperately needs.
Not an elegy. Only meteors we almost think we see.
A heart with its phone lines all tangled. Our place
in the cosmos like a seed buried in an orange. His
Gerry Mulligan, *Moonlight in Vermont,* the baritone
notes strolling through pastures, bumping into trees.
A lesson you can see on the other side of the waterfall
that you'll never understand. Not an elegy. Only this
graveyard of unfinished sentences. The scenery of a life
heaped up at the side of the stage. As when a tree falls
inside your head. As when even the atomic clocks can't
tell. All day, raindrops exploding on the windowsill.
And tonight this broken spider web, a glistening galaxy.
Perhaps the history of clouds: Lenticular, Pyrocumulus,
Noctilucent. Perhaps the history of myth,—Mot, the god
of death arriving in the Neolithic age like a desert.
Or that age when the liver was thought to be the heart.
Blind thoughts. Words asleep in the throat. A voice
over your shoulder calling you back. Blind echoes.
Francis Bacon writing that science will stop misery.
All those pink mushrooms in one spot hiding the giant
mushroom beneath the turf. The bird on that rotting
branch thinking it is a leaf. No elegy. Every elegy
in love with its speaker. No, nothing to learn from
that self-absorbed moon. Every breath an experiment.
The street singers forgetting their words that fly
off like swallows circling the chimneys and trees.
The first light falling from the sky, the first darkness

rising from the earth. The train that keeps traveling
on rails that grow impossibly narrow in the distance.
Old wagon roads the forest already claims. The wind
arriving uninvited, its needles trying to stitch you
to pure air. Impossible to calculate how many
protons pass through us each day. Colliding particles
to discover what the world was like before it was
the world. Each life a singularity no physicist could know.
No elegy. A poem with a flask in its pocket. A poem
unable to complete itself. A poem that refuses to settle
in one place. The story of the Buddha telling creation to be
patient. *A good bird can sleep on the wing.* Thus
the star-shaped prints the robin leaves in the mud.
Thus the pain of the moon that can't claw its way back up.
And this, a paper boat set on fire and gliding on
a glowing river leading nowhere. A low baritone
rippling across the water now. A lesson there, too.

Thinking About Nothing

Petroglyph NP, NM

There is nothing you can say to a friend who has died.
The night taunts us with a music we can't hear.
How does the moon reconcile itself with the branches
that cover it?

                I am looking at a symbol the Puebloans etched
into the dark face of a rock. I think these mountains are
made of wind. There's a music here that could be
the brushwork across a drum, something like the way
Alvin Stoller's pushing against the emptiness for Ben Webster
seemed to come from a day yet to appear.
                      For the Puebloans the heart was
the drum of the body.

           Birds flutter in the bushes like leaves:
it is a sound more seen than heard, the way our small histories
hide in the shade.

        There's nothing else to say unless it is the way
the light trickles into the parched earth. What these people
knew was: to see nothing so you can see what is beyond
every shape, that every stone is a window if you look
long enough.

        Michael, this was the best freedom.

The symbol here is a swirl of expanding circles
or zeros. Some say it is a reflection of the stars the way
Van Gogh drew them. Some say it is the beginning

of a story that has no end, or a story that will never be
heard again.

It was thought the Babylonians, not
these people, knowing they too would disappear into
their own desert sands, first invented a number for nothing.
In the Middle Ages, throughout Europe, zero was banned
because it was the void everyone knew as the devil.
Zechariah saw a ghostly man riding a red horse
patrolling the earth for lost souls with nothing to believe.

It doesn't take much to blindfold the heart. How easy it is
to adjust our eyes to the darkness in our own souls. We have
to believe in the hope that sleeps under the bird's wing.
There's an ancient buried river here that holds the light
of extinct stars only our radio telescopes can hear.

Why is there nothing where there should be something is
what I should be asking. The average species on earth
lives about 4 million years before its story is fossilized.
The Puebloans never wanted us to try to read these markings.

There's a huge dust devil trying to erase a distant mesa
wall of ancient lava as it has done for centuries.

Here it is like listening to the silence that trails off
into the sax after each of Ben Webster's breaths.
Wherever that silence goes the music tries to imitate.

Here we think that the edge of the universe is another
universe. A hawk burrows into the air until it is pure air.
There's nothing there except more of ourselves.

I think that's where you are now.

All or Nothing

Billie Holliday sang because she knew there was
no difference, reaching as she did beyond Stoller's drum
and Webster's sax into spaces even she didn't understand
except that, like us,

there's nothing she wouldn't have done
to hear her own lost voices, hear them breathfully, hear them
again, the way her own voice beat right out of her heart,
beat ever so lightly, to the deafened silence of the stars.

Mike Macklin, 1949-2012

Preemptive Elegy

So a time comes when the earth seems to pause in its orbit,
when a heron seems to lunge imperceptibly within itself
before taking flight over indifferent rivers. I am sleeping
between one planet and another. Over the silhouette of
your face against the window, a single star tries to fix
itself on a branch. Doesn't it know the most important
things don't exist, or don't exist yet? Each dream is a reality.

It may be eons, but the most distant photons will reach us.
So a time comes when you can hear the mortar round
searching for your soul. A time comes when the suicide
vest seems to inhale before becoming part of the fragmented
sky. The branches seem tortured by the night. Truth is
soaked up by the wind. There's a rifle shot from the hollow.
Or was it?
      Your dreams slam their doors and disappear
into the fields beyond. Will they ever exist except as Plato
thought? The candle refuses the flame. Behind each
image a past struggles to emerge. Hope swaps identity
with a nightmare. Flowers suffocate
with the latest news. A mountain rumbles
imperceptibly before it erupts. There is still time.
What doesn't exist exists more truly in words that are
about to be spoken. Each syllable is its own Psalm.
It is only inside them, inside each other, that we know
why we love.
        You call out now in your sleep. Aren't we
always someplace else waiting to take our own place?
The low bass thump of a car passes down the street
searching for an echo that won't appear. Who

do those fireflies think they are fooling when they turn
off their lights? There are so many lost lives in their eyes.
We can imagine our own deaths in another's. But
do we want to know a time when any of this ends?

A time comes when a single word assumes the shape
it names, ungraspable still, dying into meanings
that graze the heart, written only for you to read,
that little hesitation in the wind, the second thoughts
that fill our windows, the silence that grows unbearable
between your uneven breaths that I breathe as my own.

II

Avevo un bel pensiero, e l'ho perduto.
(I had a beautiful thought, but I lost it.)
                                        — *Umberto Saba*

The only thing I want to say
Glitters out of reach
Like the silver
In a pawnbroker's.

                                        — *Tomas Tranströmer*

I only arrive at the threshold of a new word.
                                        — *Clarice Lispector*

What Comes Next

There is nothing more deceptive than an obvious fact.
— Arthur Conan Doyle, "The Boscombe Valley Mystery"

There are knots of time so miserable they frighten me.
There are bodies turning into tree ornaments in Mexico.
There is the mother driving her kids into the lake
in Illinois. The antibiotics in our meat will finally kill us.
There are mornings that trudge out of the darkness
we made for them, and into the darkness we make for them.
What keeps him playing, the homeless man with his guitar
missing the bass string? He's playing *Believe it, Beloved,*
the way I remember Django Reinhardt on those scratchy
CDs. Someone drops him a coin. A robin in a dying tree
tries to answer. Sirens rake the sides of buildings.
The air has no air to breathe, the sea has no sea to define it.
There are knots of time. There are mornings. The roots
of clouds sway uncontrollably. Dreams rise up through
the chimneys. How difficult it is to write to you now.
There are shadows that deny the light that made them.
There are palms lined with regrets, hearts spotted with mold.
What am I supposed to do with the latest massacre
in Nigeria? Or the killer of a couple over a custody fight?
There are knots of time so hurtful. *Time On My Hands*
Django played so serenely he could believe in angels
gliding up and down the neck of his guitar in a melancholy
tango. In the meantime there are coffins taking the place
of forests. There's another makeshift shrine to a fallen
policeman. Are you just going to let me go on like this?
These truths appear and disappear like aging planets.
When we breathe we take in air from the farthest places
and return it to worlds that have yet to appear. Why

has it become so difficult, then, to believe in the invisible?
You might say that all of this has nothing to do with you,
or that it is simply that we are lucky to be alive, as lucky
as Reinhardt who burnt himself on his own artificial
flowers, crippling two fingers yet still went on in time
playing sudden tremolos behind Bill Coleman on *Sweet Sue*
in 1937. Which brings me back to all that fear, and so much
more we never see, but also how much meaning we never
guess is in a dot we thought was a star, but turns out to be
a galaxy of millions of stars, planets with their own secrets,
or the simple way a homeless man struggles with his own
story, waiting like all of us, for what comes next, the way
a salmon climbs a waterfall towards what it cannot see but loves.

Belief

after the freeing of the West Memphis Three

Deep in our own inner caves the heart's canary sounds a warning.
On the other side of speech is a language that dreams us.
Echoes hide out in abandoned words. The air hardens.

A home invasion, a meth lab, a father killing his family.
It Had To Be You, Les Paul played on his guitar with seven
crippled fingers, but *who* is never named, or is us.
                                                    These
clouds begin to picket the horizon. Pine sap leaks from
a wounded tree. Even the flowers seem to take on
the color of night.
                    There are times when it is better
to close your eyes to the world.

                              I have been watching
a fledgling drop from its nest, flutter a few feet, and again,
until it flew not back, but into another tree. The wind tests
itself against my torn screen. A few thorns of light jab
out of the darkness on the far hills.
                              Who are you
if your dreams are dreamt by somebody else? In a dream
of freedom we return to a place that is not the place.
                                        Orpheus'
poems could not create the world he needed. How
many times do our words become cells? How do we
remove those splinters of memory and remain ourselves?
Most of our dreams are the seeds in sidewalk cracks.

By now my fledgling has its own dream.

                              Tonight's clouds
will cover the meteor shower. I remember the fog in
the valley slipping forward like a glacier. At other times
a whole world rippled in the river.
                              It was David Hume
who said we had not a single reason to believe in reality,
but we must act as if we do. Even when a whole life
seems mothballed.
                       Now we know that our moon collided with
another moon whose remnants we can't see on its far side.
Moonglow is how Les Paul would have played it. And us?

Who are we if someone else's dream is really ours?

Letter from Slovenia

for my granddaughter, Anna Marie Thomson

I once stepped into the same river twice.
That was when I had a constellation stuck
in my throat. You were waiting on one of those
stars to be born. Today a bee's wing creates
enough wind to drench the planets. The moon
begins to untangle the shadows which
the mountain tries to tie to its cliffs. Each beat
of your heart shakes a few other stars awake.
I hope you never have to know the horrors
that cover the newspaper I am trying to write
over. Even the river pauses to listen to its own
reflections. All the children are Angels, the taxi driver
said in Baltimore last month quoting the Koran,
but in the first few weeks we all look
like the same kidney bean. I can see you
chasing butterflies and pigeons the way
your mother did. This is how my skin can hold
the memory of your touch though you should not
arrive for another week now which is exactly when
the sky will have to borrow another color
if it wants to still be the sky. You will know
your own mother as the sound of running water,
your father as the fallen petals that show
which way the water flows. When I touched
the statue of Madonna dell'Orto in Venice
for you the other day, a white chalk stuck to my hands
and I held my own clouds to the sky. What holds
the clouds up so effortlessly? Now the moss

breaks loose from the river's stones. Clouds drift
away from their roots. The river thinks
it can run uphill. Someday, when there are
only my words for you, you will hear them
as the timpani of stars. Today a hawk
flew next to the car before darting out
across the fields. I thought it was you. Each
word, each gesture, is a feather for our wings. Later,
I ran down that mountain and landed in your name.

Letter from Tuscany

for my granddaughter, Emily Frances Thomson

Inside you, a dream has begun to ignite the stems
of flowers. Now that you have arrived, this Tuscan
sky seems full of seeds. Where you are, I watched,
with your sister, a shadow that seemed to promise your shape.
The tree above me is tattooed with swallows. A few
dart around this table. I think they are memories
from your future. I think the train in the valley below is
searching, like me, to find a world that doesn't
exist yet. By then, there will be no need
to worry about the wars and tortures, the drizzle
in our hearts from this tangle of hours you'll hear about
later on. Now, even the rocky light holds
the hills in its hands. The clouds are stroking
their bald crests. I can almost slip my own arms
into the sleeves of the wind—it smudges the slender
olive leaves. Now the dark is folding the hills up
for the night. I am this happy: my pockets full of
butterflies, each breath setting off on its own
road. There's a distant smoke waiting for its fire.
The whistle is waiting somewhere for the train. I will
have to learn the language of roots. The moon's
flour covering the trees. Your words for mother,
father, sister, light, swallow, love.
The life you have before you have a life.

Leap Second

I'm having breakfast and reading the newspaper when I see
that science has added one second to our lives because
the moon's pull slows the earth's spin, making our days longer.
But because Andromeda won't come crashing into our galaxy
and swallow us all for another four billion years, the big worry is
what to do with all this extra time.

                         Think of how many seconds
have already been added to your life over the years. All those
moments like extension ladders to what you can't or don't want
to reach. You don't have to look at the doctor's report immediately.
There's no life to flash before you. Think of how many thoughts
pass through your brain in a second. How many synapses start
their own little electric storms.

                      The rain is muttering among
the fallen leaves. The fish rise but don't break the surface.
There's a man trying to catch the reflected lightning in his net.
But here, we just want the glow in the shut light's filament
to last longer.
           You can find anything in this newspaper
to fill up that extra second, anything to extend these words
though not the way time seems to hide in the spider's
woven pods or that moment we see
                    the shadow
on your mammogram, or bones going brittle, or the car
that jumped lanes to greet you, those extra moments
so unreal our daily lives waver the way the wind does
stirred by the dogwood, the way a script of smoke rises
from some cave seventy thousand years ago, trapped in one

of those extra seconds like an insect in amber, a word
in your throat, this missing page in the paper, an empty
mailbox, a heart happy not to remember but to forget.

The Secret

for Shana, getting married

What are those insect walkers called who write their secret
language on the stream's surface? Isn't all we say or see
a prism for what seems hidden. The hummingbird sees
a shade of red we have no word for. There are dozens of
earthquakes each year we never feel. There are still billions
of stars we will never name.
                              Montaigne tried to name
the power cats had to hypnotize birds out of trees, the kind
of loyalty that kingfishers showed to their injured mates
by carrying them on their backs, or the word for the way
parrot fish seemed to protect each other from fishermen.

Maybe there are names waiting for things to give them voice.
Those are the names for what any love discovers.
Even our planet is hurtling towards a space that hasn't been
created yet. We live in a world half-created by those
who know us. Inside us is another world we walk through
containing ever more worlds. There, the stars praise nothing,
the wind blows against nothing in particular unless
we notice it.
              The secret today is to know what the moonflower
knows in this false morning shade, reaching as it does towards
the morning glory across the path opening loudly towards the sun.
Between two worlds life hovers like a star, wrote Byron.
Which is why lovers live so wordlessly in each other's shade.
Which is why all comparisons like this fall short.

The shadow
of a spider looms large this morning, the language of crickets
has for a while gone extinct.
The secret is to paint your own
numbers on the clock, to brush away those webs that cover
what Stevens called *the wild country of the soul*, to let
your star hover between the flowers of the moon and the flowers
of the sun, like words you have never spoken, yet always hear.

Negative Capability

...the ability to live in uncertainty and doubt without any irritable reaching after fact or reason.
— Keats

Some days I don't know how to live. This is not about that.
It doesn't matter that there are a few snarled thunderstorms
to the south, a few nails of light hammering the hills to the north.
I'm sitting on the impossibly spherical space of a Reiman
universe where straight lines are curved, where nothing ever
ends or begins, and amid the invisible village of Lidice razed
by the Nazis, everyone killed or deported, even the trees, even
the old graves uprooted. I'm sitting in a rose garden that is
no longer a street, where no longer the lamppost lights
a nameless man who once played his bandaged sax to the moon.

How do you measure what's lost when it's no longer there?
I imagine he plays *Round Midnight* though he couldn't
know it the way Sonny Rollins did in 1996, pausing, diving
deeper, floating across the surface then sinking to a kind of
moan. It's what I am listening to now, the sax trying to say
it has nothing to do with what happened here, apologizing.
In fact, this is not about anything until you say it is. We assume
a reader who understands, but there's nothing to understand
here. The sky hides the sky, stars hide other stars. But this is
not about any of that, because so much has been distorted
to make it sound like an easy truth. There's no way to defend
ourselves against these nightmares. Not today with a killer
shooting children at a Peace Camp in Norway, another shooting
into a skating rink in Dallas.

But this is not about any of that
either. Some roses have wilted, others start to bloom. Every
memorial tries to say what can't be said. Maybe I should listen
to the hidden bird on the side of one of these ghost trees.
I wish he would replace the clock. But today even our own
footprints seem outlawed. There are warehouses of emotion
we rarely touch, piles of newspapers with no front page,
mirrors refusing reflections. Sometimes our shadows shiver
without us. Sometimes tomorrow falls on yesterday. This is
not about the reefs of stars our hopes are dashed upon, not
our splintered skies, however true, though one story always
reflects another. I mean, this has nothing to do with memory,
which is never enough. Our lives are just a sideshow here.
This is not about the flight of crows passing through my soul.
There shouldn't be a way to say anything here that will last,
no way to start again. Every pier ends in failure. I think it has
something to do with the heads of the unborn that turn away.
Sometimes we call to them, and sometimes we see more
when we look through a spider's web. Why does a single tear
weigh more than the earth?
             All our memories are rubble
no one can rebuild. I don't know what they sing, the angels
haunting these fields. And who could listen to Sonny Rollins
that way I do now among this orchestra of bullets still spitting
into the earth from another age. Sometimes we are amazed
just to find that we are still alive, as the whole world begins
to move in the light of a paused note, and I begin to write this,
the roses stammering, the group of 49 bronze girls and 42
bronze boys scanning the valley as if they entered our thoughts,
which is why they are still so worried, the levees of language
failing, the heart floundering, the world disappearing into an
endless tune that waits for the nothing we must always become.

Sifting

*In me every thought, however much I like to preserve it
intact, turns sooner or later into reverie.*
— *Pessoa,* A Notebook that Never Was

for Iztok Osojnik

There must be an idea around here someplace, maybe
something left like those prayers tucked into crevices
on gravestones, or the torn-out pages of a phone book,
though it's possible they've all been blown away by
the solar wind that ate the atmosphere of Mercury
and is nibbling on ours. Some ideas descend like the god
Mercury who brought fresh ideas to the ancients.
Sometimes he took a little detour from the truth.
Nothing shows up on the radar, the sonar whispers ghosts.
Come on, even plants have ideas, or why else would
Brussels sprouts send messages for wasps to eat the eggs
deposited by cabbage butterflies, or willow roots strangle
pipe lines for water?

                Sometimes our words are so many
versions of Christ, parables no one wants to hear.
Stevens thought the best ideas were found on garbage
dumps. Odysseus searched for ten years and never found
an idea he could love. On the other hand, Newton had to wait
for an apple to fall. And what about those apostles with
tongues of flame above their heads? There's inspiration
for you.

          Sometimes our ideas sneak out and have strange
encounters with other ideas we don't recognize. A few
rejected ones drag themselves out of the mind's trapdoor.
Some are so far out and scattered they become part of

the outer asteroid belt that threatens us. For example,
the other day I was peeling carrots but couldn't get the word
triangulate out of my head, and then every sax player
who ever recorded *Willow Weep for Me*. Okay, a lot of
ideas are meant to be swept under the rug. Sometimes we have
to ask if any idea is just or true if it can't prevent things
like three-year-old refugee Sarah Jahirovic's three heart
attacks from the lead slag heap the UN abandoned above her
Gypsy camp near Mitrovica, Kosovo.

But we want to forget
what doesn't fit into our window frames. We want their harsh
light to fizzle out like damp fireworks. Even Christ's ideas
have been twisted like smoke in the wind. Sometimes we want
our ideas to be ideals, like those little train-set towns, the gate
lowering each time the train comes around. There must be a million
of those ideas around here. Sometimes their horror seems
calming like the ideas of the Mitrovica children who are waiting
to turn into the gray lead dust that rubs their air. But you are
not supposed to think about these things. We tie time in knots
then watch it all unravel. Plato thought everything came down
to one idea. Loneliness is contagious, wrote Pavese, but
who would you give it to? What I really want, Iztok says,
is an idea that can't be thought. Only by imagining something
do we see how real it is.

One idea rubbernecks after
another that's failed. Like the idea of the Gypsy camp in Lety,
Czechoslovakia that the Nazis ran and is echoed
now in Kosovo. Or the other camps that have fallen into
memory's roadside ditches. This morning I watched
the last star being erased by the swaying branch

of an English oak. Someone says half the stars are cloned.
Raindrops are melted stars. Snakes are frozen lightning.
Therefore my next idea will have to be revised even before
it appears. Ideas are porous. Victims evaporate in the sun.
We have to triangulate despair and cruelty with our own
translated feelings. Even now the sky is reevaluating
the idea of sky. No star knows what the other is thinking.

Sometimes too many ideas roam the other side of this page.
Aren't all our horizons inside us? Each death takes shelter
in another. Each idea is a refugee crossing someone's border.
Some ideas are like bodies frozen under the ice before being
revived a few hours later. Still others think we don't
need to exist. They shove other ideas into boxcars and camps.
Some ideas sift down like lead dust. The brain hopes that
if it doesn't think of it, it doesn't exist. What were we thinking?
These deceitful clouds never tell the same story. The dictionary
of loss is hopelessly beyond us. I don't think the sky can be
held accountable anymore. This is the prayer I placed on the grave.
The center of the universe, said Pascal, is wherever you are.
There's a dog from one of those camps barking at the edge
of my sleep, but he never enters. Some ideas have no windows.
Sometimes when we look at something, said Iztok, it is not actually
there. The dog's howling raises a tuft of dust on the moon.
That's the whole idea, at least as far as I understand it.

Everything All at Once

There's a buck beyond the far end of the field
but he doesn't know he's dying, couldn't know,
that is, the patience behind the sights he's caught in.
The dignity of just being alive, the freedom of it.
So many sounds coming from the grass and the trees.
On the farm further past the woods a finger of smoke
desperate for a word to contain it. A few dilapidated
clouds. We have come here following a map from
memory. The horizon refuses to go on. You can feel
the sun as it flees. How is it we feel the need to lose
what we love? There's a star or a planet just starting
to shudder behind the leaves as if to deny the darkness.
You can hear the buck knock its knees together
then urinate on them, rubbing it in, to attract whatever
doe is nearby. He won't come into the field just yet.
How many times have we practiced our own deaths?
Our truths seem as packaged as these bales of hay.
A hundred and fifty years ago two armies slaughtered
themselves here. Maybe that is what the buck senses.
Far beyond that horizon a woman looks into the bomb
crater that was her home. It is the last word in
a sentence of many words. She could live on any map.
The early mapmakers created worlds that put them
at the center. One described the earth as a yolk
in an eggshell. Believe me, it is that delicate.
Aren't our first words names for what we don't have
or have lost? Don't we want everything all at once?
The light's shredding. There's still time to fire.
What is there to feel but the way sometimes we seem
safe and something in our own voice surprises us

to see we cared more than we expected. The buck
hides inside his own meaning. The silence of the hawk
just overhead seems to stop time. Some words are
wounds that do more damage than a shot that rings out.

Is This the Person to Whom I Am Speaking

In the end is my beginning.
— *T.S. Eliot*

All I need to begin is a first line and, well, there it is.
Sometimes things just begin like that fatherless species
of lizard in the desert Southwest. Sometimes the moment
you don't want arrives utterly uninvited. Like all these
ladybugs, where do they come from? Not every sky is
reflected in the puddle. Not every love wanders in to stay.
The mockingbird in our tree is rebuilding its nest.

Are you talking to yourself? Yes I'm talking to my selves.
Sometimes we're just an echo of what we meant to say.
"Do you mean your reality or mine," Brittain once said.
But how would we ever know if we didn't exist?
Sometimes we are just ideas from someone's head the way
Athena sprung from Zeus. Think about it: if corn oil
comes from corn, where does baby oil come from?
Do you see how difficult it is to strike the right tone?

No one knows where those people buried under boats
in the Chinese desert came from. Four thousand years
ago they marked their graves with huge phallic poles.
Should that intimidate me, you ask. "I was born dead,"
wrote Chagall. Each image in his paintings destroys
another image. Sometimes I think of you as his Bella
floating over the kitchen table as if she were an angel
or mockingbird.
              By the way, how did they get Christ
to sit for all those portraits? Fruit flies provide a lesson
here: they destroy their own memories so they can

get on with their brief lives. And by now you realize
there is no story here.

             Wordsworth said a poet
begins in gladness but ends in madness, which I include
here for the cheap rhyme, and because, well, I like it.
Once you begin the trick is to keep going. We are all
refugees from time as long as we can keep talking.
The point is to keep gathering these bits and scraps.

Some things never last. A duck's quack doesn't echo.
The letters my uncle Bernard wrote before his B-17
tumbled into Belgium have long since been hijacked.
Dale likes Belgian beer. The earthquake in Chile
shifted the earth's axis by three centimeters so we are
all slightly tilted from the other day. I'm feeling dizzy.

Who ever notices these small changes? While the ditches
in Bosnia were being filled with mutilated bodies
flowers bloomed the brightest in years, birds sang to
exquisite heights. Now, the puddle wrinkles like an old
man's skin.

             "My blood is too scared to leave my body,"
said Erin. The stars drop like lures. Flowers empty
their cups. The grass is gullible. The earth keeps on
trembling. Everything dies, sang Springsteen. Even
coral fight each other by spitting poison. Dung beetles
fight over the eggs they've wrapped in dung, much
like us. That is an imge meant to evoke death but who
has experienced it? Every death is a secret. The thing is
not to finish.

On the other hand, pike fish mate for thirty
minutes every ten days just before dawn. Cuttlefish
screw faster than anything alive. But this raises again
the question of how to keep going in between so you
never face an endgame.

        Dear heart, this is what I've been
trying to do all these years, and lines. Sometimes I think
I could become the wind. Even Nicodemus didn't have
any faith until he believed in metaphor.

        Sometimes
my words fray at their ends. Sometimes their candles
burn down. Their meanings are those ghosts or angels
we catch in the corner of our eyes, a reality that never
quite stays, never leaves. They float like the clouds
of egg and sperm released by coral when they are
not trying to destroy each other. They hang below
the surface like Chagall's lovers. Chagall knew
the real is what you paint bit by bit. His lovers are
sheathed by the wind.

        All we need to avoid an ending is
a line that promises its own future. The mockingbirds have
taken, just now, the string you hung out for their nests.

The Storm

A little gene turns rebellious and a little switch
gets turned off in the brain along with most of
memory. The older we get the more we fear
such revolts. You can't just press the rewind
button in your mind. For a moment the sky
exhales and it's

            Pisgah Mountain, NC, 2011,
a tide of clouds slowly shrouding the summit.
It's headed this way, pushing memories in front
of it like a negligent driver missing one of
the hairpin turns here. You can measure the fog
by the way the wind shoves it around until
the storm arrives.

            Or the fog in Sarajevo, 1987,
Tatyana Nisic, long leather coat made of night,
leading the way to the cellar Speak Easy before
the war, before the snipers playing cards for
the next shot.
            Like lightning, there's the flash
and then a woman drops.

            Or you watching
the whirligig turn counterclockwise as if to imitate
the approaching tornado, wires and lives starting
to snap, ourselves stumbling deep into another cellar.
The wind so loud we never hear the trees falling.

Now a few far mountain lights shout through the fog.
It must signal the storm clambering up the other side.
The distant heat lightning has no point of origin.
The mountain seems to be fighting against itself.

Maybe the present is itself a road with no signs.
What we fear is a world that has been mothballed.
What you must understand is that this is a love poem.
I can't walk down deep enough into the wind.

Misunderstood

I should tell you from the start that this poem is about Nothing.
Even the title is stolen from a song by Wilco. It's true
that some philosophers say that Nothing exists, except in dreams,
that our words carry meanings like the hidden roots of stars,
that ideas flake off the walls of our metaphors like old paint.
My own dreams are full of riots.

                              Sartre said Nothingness is
the basis of all Being. Every word is a signpost on an empty
road. Shadows rebel. Flames rise like antlers. Lives float by
like bodies on a river.

                              Where are we going with this? When
the band's notes flew off in wrong directions, Charlie Mingus
just fired a few players and started again. Me too.

                                                    Time
opens its doors to whoever knocks. In this case the *Honest
Pint* in Chattanooga, TN. Inside there's another lively
discussion about whether God exists if he permits such evil,
but I have nothing to say about it or the recent bombing
on the rail line Dostoevsky's Idiot Prince took to St. Petersburg,
or about the four policemen shot in Seattle, or the soldiers
at Fort Hood.

                    The wind gnaws through the space where
the bones of the tree once hung. The past is a horizon
made of more horizons. There's nothing we can do. In Sarajevo
a girl looks out through the hole where her bedroom wall
used to be and sees a world she doesn't want to see.

                                                    The wind
chimes at my window are full of senseless interpretations.
The flower is still trying to understand the stem. The clocks
have their own opinions. One day catapults into the next.

The idea that suffering might not have any meaning is
what haunts me. Even now too many things surface and pass
before I can understand them. Even the moon doesn't understand
what we've made of her. I say *her* as if to claim her for my own,
but everything lives in the emptiness of its absence.

Don't you have something better to do?

How many emotions
have already vacated our hearts? The world is a nest of absences.
Every once in a while someone comes along to fill the gaps.
Overhead, satellites are mapping our dreams. The stars look
right through us. The owl is meditating on the existence
of mice. Evil exists because the blade of the moon cuts through
the parchment of the sky. It persists like the odor in a dead
man's room.
        Now I see I have written myself into Schrödinger's
box and have to guess at my own existence. This is the anguish
of dying galaxies too distant to see. The space we might fill
tomorrow is already closing.

There's not much time left to say
something, as Blake's character tells another at the end
of *Jerusalem*. This is why I have written you in here, hoping
to find a way to change the meanings of these words, to say
war but mean peace, death but mean life, hate but mean your love,
nothing but mean everything you could possibly mean to be.

Another Small Apocalypse

That twenty thousand people in the early 19th century
watched twenty-three animals, including a bear, ride over
Niagara Falls in a burning mock pirate ship tells us
something about who we are.
                            It is either night or
ashes from some distant tragedy floating in the air.

It's not the horror but the horror's face we must imagine
as our own. We can't bandage our hypnotized hearts.
We like to carve our names on rocks, in trees, as if
by this we owned them.
                            Excuses fill the night
like bats. This is why we need so many distractions—
Twitter, Facebook, texting—anything to stop thinking.

It's why Lot's wife turned back to gaze at her own death.

It's as if our souls lined up like pigeons on telephone wires.
Or that we thought a plane's unreachable vapor trail held
our innermost secrets.
                            We believe in dogmas we don't
understand. Someone wears a bomb into a mosque
and we hardly have time to mourn before the next
commercial. Our days walk by unconcerned. Night
covers up the names of the lost.
                            Here, we watch the owl
watching for prey. The treed opossum hangs in the tree
all night, afraid, waiting for us to move on. The lake
refuses to shimmer. The lava of our lives hardens.

A few lightning bugs try to warn us. I remember someone
saying most poems only watch like old men gazing quietly
at the tide. Even our memories seem like retouched photographs.
Our words hang ill-fitting in the closet.
                                                There are still
9,000 unidentified bones from 9/11.

                                        If you listen closely
you can hear this poem trying to find a way out of these
nightmares. I write this on a moonless night, the birds
inexplicitly quiet, watching the onlookers gather at
the yellow tape of another murder lit by the flash of cameras.

Facebook

Ginny found a wounded stallion in Farmville and wants you
to give it shelter for the night. Hannah's hands feel like two
water balloons. Andy noticed Christ's return is set for May 21,
2011. Sophie is riding the tail of a comet. Peter thinks he was
once an exploding Nebula. Mary sees her soul spread out
across the Milky Way. Reggie just can't take it anymore.
Melody really isn't here. V's new boyfriend's girlfriend is
V's mother who is over her own affair with her new boyfriend's
friend's friend. Pictures to follow. 7 people like this. Rick
watched someone steal coins from a fountain in Prague.
The sky has fallen on Jennifer. Joan's heart has narrow streets.
Happy Birthday, Pricilla, and no, the other drunks don't know
when you're drunk. 35 people ignored her invitation. Me, too.
Should I apologize? Make up an excuse? Continue to ignore her?
These are just impulse buys waiting in a line to check out.
Elizabeth lost her heart but found it under a shot glass.
Mark is having chaos for dinner. Robin killed a groundhog
to save her plants. So many moral dilemmas. Jane made
dinner. Paul woke up late. Marilyn walked the dog. Adam
commented on Daniel's Status. Lana wants to recall everyone.
Today in 1567 Mary Queen of Scots abdicated. "The future
begins in the large intestine," wrote Milorad Pavić. We are
made up of so much water we can't swim out of ourselves.
Besides, all the readers of this page are entirely imaginary.
All we have are these rings of keys for which there are
no doors. Jessie is watching the arthritic hands of the clock.
She's not coming back, Jessie. The crows are raising a racket.
Maybe we are all blind salamanders living in endless caves.
What we mean is how lonely we are, how desperate for a life.
How nice that someone is rummaging through your profile!

Roger has three gifts for you. Maura has risen new heights
in Mafia Wars. Duck, there's a cream pie coming at you.
It's time for your status update. Please let us know. Carolyn
poked John who poked Mary who poked you who poked
Carolyn who withdrew her poke. There are three dead trees
perilously close to my house. The odds on someone proving
the existence of God are now set at 100-1. Beth wants to know
how to get rid of her memories without killing herself. That's
a tough one, Beth. Here's a painting of David holding Goliath's
head which is a self-portrait of Caravaggio. We are so many
versions of ourselves. I have 617 friends so far. I've tagged you
with a cobweb of photos. Was it worth it, Peter? There's
a voice you hear in your dreams you think is real. "Around
the same time, someone is walking, far from here, away
from here, with no plans of coming back," Bolano wrote
in *Antwerp* which, like this, has no real plot. "Cleaning utensils
began to levitate in her head," he says. The wind lifts the dust
from the road. Is it bad manners to refuse being *friended*?
Pam and Bill watched the Perseids scratch the sky last night.
That's what prompted the coyotes' lament. It stays pasted
to the sky. Isn't this like a movie where the projectionist has
fallen asleep. Does Laurie ever get off of this page? Melody
refuses to vacate the premises. Oh for those old TV *Sign Off*
signals. The grass is growing out of control. The paint's chipped.
The bills haven't been paid. Sleep nudges my door but it's locked
shut. Peter wants to be friends so he can appear in this poem.
Who doesn't. Too bad, Peter, the poem's already over.

Tip of My Tongue

I forget what I was going to say but it was right there on
the tip of my tongue,

                        but if I keep on here it's sure to come
back to me like one of those women we thought had been
sawed in half during those old vaudeville acts.

                                        But the thing is,
not all that we remember is helpful, as when the Herald
in *Agamemnon* starts to remind the crowd about all their
dead who won't return from Troy and so they begin to turn
on him, until he stops mid-fragment and changes direction.

Or you might end up like Plato's chattering crickets whose
meaning is only background,

                              or your own prattle might mean
too much like one of the *disappeared* who were abducted,
wined or dined into a stadium in Santiago where, as the joke
went, the wine turned back into blood.

                                    The thing is to sift out
the important sounds, little syllables and vowels that bring
hints of their lost words, and not to mistake the fossil for
the life, or the kiss for the love, not to mistake the fragment
for the sentence.

                          The thing is, we scrape our dreams on a word
we never saw, or wander around in the empty rooms
of our souls looking for words to define ourselves just as
God wandered around Eden out of loneliness, or as Jimmy
Piersal tried to hide behind the flag pole at Fenway Park
unable to say where he was.

The thing is we get there eventually
once we stop thinking about what we are thinking about, unless
someone takes the words out of our mouths,

                                    though in this case
I am remembering now the word for what was described, how the grenade
seemed to pause for a moment before painting its gaudy colors
on the sky, like the several suns coming into being in any moment
in the universe, remembered in the impossibly beautiful, impossibly
horrifying sentences no one could say, no one could remember.

My Many Disguises

I'll be there in no time, you said, which would make
waiting a thing of the past except that time wouldn't exist.
Sometimes we just want to be those ancient insects trapped
forever in amber. We want to know about that tree
growing down into the seabed off Norfolk, England, about
the next life the ancient Beaker people planted it to grow
towards.

      We want to know where the Door to Eternity
with its concentric carved frames unearthed in Luxor,
Egypt, leads to. Even the evening comes on as if it didn't
understand what it is doing. Maybe that's why we say
the evening is so melancholy, for it reminds us that we are
the only species that knows there's a last breath waiting
for us, and because the dead, sadly, have no need of us.

Look, even cockroaches can live nine days without their heads.
Euripides thought every god lives inside us as an unspoken word.
That's why we become whatever we imagine, the way
hover flies disguise themselves as wasps or bees so
nothing will attack them. Everything wants to live forever
but even the sun is slowly dying out. Everything wants to be
something else. Same difference, as the saying goes, but in fact
everyone's watch shows a different time. I'm not sure but
I think these details will be important later on.

      Fireflies signal
their mates with a unique Morse Code of flashes. I wish
I could tell you everything, but each memory is an aftershock
sending the old truths scurrying over rotting thresholds
of belief, and into dimly lit side streets. In fact, I'm not sure
how you feel about being in here, though you are only

a pronoun. In the end we all become a name someone
else also has.
                    Maybe no one hears our cries simply
because we speak a language of extinct hearts.
The call of a humpback whale can be heard for 500 miles.
The heart of a blue whale is as big as a small car.
                                            The old
wrecks in the abandoned lot have turned into dead stars.
Maybe those scientists who created artificial bacteria can help.
The wind leaves a puzzle in the dust from demolished buildings.
It doesn't matter that the moment is always splintered wood.

What comes next appears like a number at the deli counter.
We never know where the paths of the wind begin or end.
It doesn't matter how many rocks we throw against the hour.
Sometimes we hold each other as if we were the thinnest clouds.
We are just minor characters in someone's forgettable novel.

If the alley is deep enough you can see whole constellations.
Maybe people have the same kind of attraction as binary stars
that eventually collide and destroy each other. Sometimes
they just go whirligigging into other galaxies. Isn't that why
we are made of stardust and interstellar light? Doesn't
every love set off the security lights in the heart?
You just have to know the difference between true and
magnetic north. Every word here stands for a star I have
kidnapped.
                    The latest theory is that the universe is made up
of bits of information so that we are just chips in some
giant computer. To someone light years away we are

just a tiny blue dot made up of the wrong chemicals.
I don't know whether this is the beginning or the middle.
I don't even know if I want to continue with this, or if
everything just dies when I'm done. How would I know?

There's a bit of leftover sun blowing around on the corner.
There's the quivering branch the robin has just left.
Nothing is complete until we can see it. Even the trees
hold their breath. It may seem forever until you arrive.
There's the prison of my shadow, these words which are
roadblocks, their elliptical emotions, the night's refusals.

It may mean the dead need us, after all, to say the unsayable,
to hold in our hands a simple rose, to cup the wind, to feel
the endless longing the heart brings back from its inverted
world, a feeling that has no metaphor for what it is.

III

By now the moon itself is blue. By this
We mean that we can see in it the full freight
Of our unspent love for it, for the blue night,
And for the hour, which is late.

—William Matthews

Yet you live somewhere else.

— Cesare Pavese

What doth this noise of thoughts within my heart
As if they had a part.

— George Herbert, "The Family"

Not Here, Not There

Shrimp's hearts are in their heads. All of our light is
made of protons that began someplace that is no longer
where it was. There's a man selling postcards from
the Rapture. Leonardo's *Battle of Anghiari* is probably
hidden behind Vasari's great painting in Florence's city hall.
Who is going to occupy this space when we are gone?

Here is only this park, green, peopled with memories.
No one knows why one of the stars of Orion is shrinking.
A farmer plows up a decades-old bomb manufactured on
another continent. Is it true that everything comes from
nothing? Everything we believe arrives on brain waves
made of calcium and carried by astrocytes.
                              Sometimes
we leave our feelings in the mirror for the next person
to put on. Our promises wander among our dying neurons.
The distant ridges seem to push against the sky.
Memories fade like worn names on tombstones.

When they throw acid on the faces of the Afghan girls
for attending school it is to keep them from learning of
other places, frightening beliefs.
                       And here, wherever
here is, in a solar system itself always on the move?
Here I never know how many beats are left in my heart.
Here there is the simple curve of your hips, the most
sensual thing I know. Here my hopes sit like refugees
in my mind. With each breath we leave part of the soul
behind. The boys gliding over the field to sail their kites
know none of this. The late shadows cover the grass
like fallen trees. Rags of light flicker beyond the ridge.

Where are we going? The disciples asked Jesus, but where
He was going they couldn't follow. We want to follow
each other the way we follow and hold these images.
There's something that we know but can't name, what
follows the fading song of the late light, what the boys'
kites carry, lifted by distant winds towards heights
I can hardly imagine, breaths that follow miraculously.

Living On

I can't imagine dying because the Amazon Candiru, a kind of
tiny catfish, swam up, as it did one man standing just offshore,
his urine stream and into his penis,

                                 or its monster cousin, Asu,
the *driller killer* that burrows into flesh and eats your inner organs.
Another catfish, the Giant Goonch from the Kali River in India,
can swallow a man whole.
                         There are just too many ways to die—
Sherwood Anderson swallowing a toothpick or Isadora Duncan
getting her famous scarf caught on the wheel of the car she was in.

Death Takes A Holiday the movie goes, but it's a lie. It's Time's
rusty pliers that pull at us. That's why Augustine mourned
a time before the beginning of the world where time didn't exist,
which now our scientists confirm.

                           But no, Death just goes to work
like a draft through a window jamb, or the monster at the window
that we just miss.

                  Therefore, the way to live is to know what you will
forget.

        Here the drought starts to drink the air. The sun reaches
down for us like a mythic monster. At night we let the stars lie
about their temperatures. Even our dreams turn brown. The future
falls out like sediment.

In the end we all pray for something,
if only the need for no prayer whose words continue on
somewhere in the future.

The dove on the inner branch watches me
as if to ask a question. We all have answers for questions
we can't express.

The birds that sing all night pray for whatever
we have forgotten or ignored, today for Ali Ferzat, 60, whose
drawings helped depose several dictators, whose hands were broken
by Syrian loyalists as a warning, and who lives on with his art
against the monsters.

I don't have to imagine how the grass waves
desperately, trees shed their bark, the cicada leaves its shell,
and the heart walks out of Fear's mythical, impenetrable desert.

Endurance

for Sebastian, after the wreck

A few deer pause inside the rain, more gauze
than rain, and hear with their eyes the no-sound
we make. Darkness starts to collect the darkness
and sprinkles it among the deadfall behind them.
And behind that, a ravine filled with rusting washers
and waiting stories.
          Clouds hide the tumult
inside them.
          I don't even know what I was
thinking.
          It is not hard to imagine how quickly
we'll be forgotten. What endures is the idea we can
endure. We hang these stories on a few fragile
branches of memory.
          This is where you are
supposed to be addressed with allusions to
the particulars.
          We are alive because each of us
owns a word we keep trying to pronounce.
I must go in, the fog is rising, Dickinson said
before being "called home." You'd think the rain
might mend a bruised heart. We can't even complete
the sentences of our lives.
          Now the deer disappear
and leave behind instructions for later, their trails

almost imperceptible. The rain thins so it can return
later to the clouds. It is hard to tell whether it is
mist or fog. Or the collecting gray. Or mere distance.

Not until there is that single word that reaches deep
into our lungs and pulls out the last, enduring breath.

Out of Place

Škocjan, Slovenia

It takes a while for the moon to pull itself up
over the Karst hill planed down by the wind.
It doesn't suspect anything of the anvil of
clouds that will flatten it like so many lives here.
Darkness drips from the rooftop gutters.
No one bothers about the desperate echo
of a hunter's gun coming up from the woods.
No one here wants to remember the war.
The few last birds abandon the telephone wire.
It's a remorseful moon that spreads out
like milk over the pasture. The horses there
have not come in and are still chewing on
the sweet karst grass. No matter what language
the owl speaks, there is no answer that satisfies us.
A few last bits of conversation circle each other
like dying stars. Our words are geodes.

On the other side of this page the moon is held
in the ribs of the sky. Around the two horses
the palm print of a cloud seems to press down
on the stalks, and they follow it as if it were
a call to move. One is white, the other gray,
a metaphor for the two-tone cloud above them.
It's on this side that the moon becomes the heart.
It's there that you become the late hawk riding
a wind that has come from beyond the moonrise,
become a tiny shadow of a field mouse among
the twigs waiting to scamper back to its burrow
as well as the hawk itself, become grass, horse,

shadow, part of the swoop where the mouse has been lifted up, becoming sky. It's on that side that I remember that all our skies are inside us. All our worlds are self-portraits.

Jacob's Fear

I have lived too long as a prisoner of clouds.
They float like clothes strung over the barbed wire
from one of your camps, a story that has no words.
I don't even know if these dreams are my own.
What I know is based on what is not there: a shadow
behind a wavering curtain in a fifth-floor walk-up,
a mirror filled with disbelief, the dark spaces
between stars. What is it that any of us fights with
except what betrays us, and what betrays us is
what we are. My own sons knew nothing but revenge
for their sister and wiped out a town. There is a shame
that is the hidden face of the world. It is all betrayal.
All we can do is limp through history. Every bone is
a kind of crutch. After a while I became only a few words
scribbled to mean whatever you want them to mean.
Sometimes I believe the only truths worth reading are
spray-painted on overpasses and the rocky sides of hills.
The afternoon walks through fields like a farmer whose
crops have failed. This is not what you wanted to hear,
and frankly, you need a kind of stage manager to keep
all this straight. I too once thought our dreams escaped
to inhabit other souls when we died. I too thought that
the bodies at Babi Yar, arranged so efficiently so as not
to have to dig too deep, was a moment, a displaced
fragment of history. One time I knew exactly what to do.
One time I thought it was just God's punishment
the way your preachers justify bombings and tornadoes,
or the gassing of whole Syrian or Kurdish villages,
as something deserved. How perverse to excuse
one nightmare with another. Who would want that God?

Now I am just tired of revenge. Why should our words be
indictments, our lives summarized on police blotters.
Time is tired of being time. What does the fish think
as it leaves the water, and the insect at that very moment?
Does it matter that this is the only mystery worth knowing?
Each millennium the planets create a new geometry of the sky.
The question is, will any of this change us. Will it stop
the stars from turning their backs on us? Once, back then,
they changed my name, but I left a shadow there. Now
I am afraid our dreams wait, quivering, hanging from skies
like those bats infected with fungus in caves we can't explore.

Abraham's Journey

Sorrow walked in my clothes before I did. Flocks
of shadows followed me. One night I looked at the stars
I thought were gods until they disappeared. Some say
I smashed my father's idols and walked away.
Or walked towards a desert of barren promises.
Or promises that are hummingbirds hovering for
a moment then drifting away. Even now, walking
towards that mountain, sometimes I will watch
my shadow sitting beneath a plane tree, casting dice,
ignoring my steps. Some of you made me a founder
but it was only that shadow. Some of you made me
your father, but it was yourselves you were describing.
You plant a tree, you dig a well, and it brings life,
that's all. Everything else is the heart's mirage.
Except what begins inside you. Except Sarah.
When she stepped inside my dream the curtains
shivered, whole mountains entered the room.
It always seemed a question of which love to honor.
The land I loved fills with fire. Who should we listen to?
It's true, He offered the world and I offered only
myself. But I thought His words were coffins. I was
frantic for any scrap of shade. Now everything is
shade. Your old newspapers are taken up by the wind
like pairs of broken wings. Each window, each door is
a wound. One track erases another track. One bomb.
One rock, one rubber bullet. What can I tell you?
Where have you left your own morning of promises?
You remember Isaac, maybe Ishmael, but not the love
that led me there. Not Sarah. Just to hear the sound
of her eyelids opening, or her plants pushing the air

aside as they reach for the sun, twilight filling
her fingers like fruit. This afternoon a flock of doves
settled on my porch. Their silence took the shape
of all I ever wanted to say. Today, the miracle
you want aches inside the trees. Why believe
anything except what is unbelievable? I never
thought of it as a trial, not any of it. Now the leaves
turn into messages that are simply impossible to read.
The roots turn into roads as they break through
the surface. How can I even know what I mean?
Beneath the hem of night the rain falls asleep
on the grass. We have to turn into each other.
One heart inside the other's heart. One love. One word.
Inside us, our shadows will walk into water,
the water will walk into the sky. Blind. Faithful.
Inside us the music turns into a flock of birds.
Theirs is a song whose promise we must believe
the way the moon believes the earth, the fire believes
the wood, that is, for no reason, for no reason at all.

Isaac's Consent

Why did the silence lay heavy on his shoulder?
Why did the animals we passed close their eyes in shame?
For a while the land had no horizon. For that while
he never trusted me, never thought I might consent.
We never see the storms loitering behind the mountains
with almost too much to say. For three days
I carried the bowl of fire. I watched the locusts
clinging to their blades of grass. On the first day,
there was a small boy, puzzled, who thought
he could put the morning moon in a bucket.
On the second day, a beggar slipped off his stool
because he knew the answers to everything
I asked. On the third, I knelt on the wood pile.
The ram caught in the bushes was no concern of mine.
We only see what we want to see, hear what we want to hear.
The prisoners you mistreat are no concern of yours.
Everyone is a victim. No difference. Even today, your soldiers
talk to a blind Tomorrow that disappears down some
sniper alley, or turns its back on them, or plants
a roadside mine. Even your flags can't be trusted.
One missile goes astray and several futures join
the long history of collateral damage.
I wanted only that there be no more lies.
I wanted my father, and you, to say what you mean.
To find a word for our faith older than faith.
Does the future always have to flash like a knife?
Do we always have to create dreams from our histories?
What escapes you, never leaves you. Everything is
a journey of trust. You have to have the kind of faith

the flame has for the candle, that the bird has for its wings.
Otherwise, our words have no destinations.
Otherwise, our words are snakes that swallow our souls.
Today, I heard the river empty itself of its memories.
I knew I would have to tell you all of this.
I think I could speak with the voice of the ram.

Certainty

No one knows why it happened that way and not
the other way. No one knows why the words of the story
changed their meanings so suddenly. There was a road, yes,
but no one wanted to take it. A considerable wind
combs through the mist but reveals nothing. Feedback
has been nonexistent. Only the regrets of doorways
and the conscience of violins. So typical. You can monitor
the fault lines, measure the compression between tectonic
plates, but it only tells you something after the fact.
Like the way history is the record of forgotten soldiers
a farmer digs up, or a landmine a child forfeits a limb
to see. No one knows why *today imitates yesterday* is
what the trees whisper to one another. Imagine the people
who wonder what we are doing in their parallel world.
No one knows what the constellations really looked like
millions of years ago. I'm tired of pushing this shopping
cart of old meanings. What ever happened to the love
poems I was writing? The latest estimate is that we are
descended from only 18,500 people. Why did the sun
rise so half-heartedly today? No one wants to put training
wheels on the heart. How long are you going to sit there
and let me go on like this? No one understands what
the liquid on one of Saturn's moons is made of. Broccoli
was the source of Descartes' intense meditations on God.
You can see traces of his thought everywhere like those
lines that mark the destroyed nests of mud wasps.
No one knows if the moon's half-erased craters means
it was once our shield against meteors. Its mountains are
devoted to their dark ravines. The sun is about to set.
There's a bird caught in my chimney again. No one else

has visited tonight. You could hear your eyelids shut.
Does it really matter what anybody else knows?
Pascal thought everything we know is a metaphor.
Plato thought everything we know is already inside us.
I am going to tell you about everything with certainty,
Democritus said, but then changed the subject.
No one knows the distance between love and Love.
One time, your heart almost slipped away on a river
barge. Your hands seemed to claw the sky. I'm sorry.
No one else made anything out of those streaked clouds.
The fact that it happened is proof enough for me.
And then it was like the starlight I feel on my skin,
like the molten lava the earth's crust slides across.
The dead branches of the tree wander off into the air
like dried-out river beds. So it happens that what
we know is the space the broken arm of the statue
should occupy, meaning what it must point to, but
no one knows, no one ever knows, what to call it.

Walking the Dog

Should I worry when I say one thing but mean another?
Black sap drips from the trees. Sleeves of wind sway
like branches. Just beyond here the road falls into doubts.
Leaves are beginning to migrate. My dog measures the world
by sniffs. I measure it by how many things I can do at once.
I don't think I have ever lived in one place at a time.
I think the workmen across the street are hanging gutters
to collect the sunlight. The older one has a face of twine.
Shadows of birds skim across the windows beneath them.
Coming up the hill the joggers seem to lean against the air.
Nice dog, but they don't mean it. They're afraid she'll bite.

No one really says what they mean. Iztok says everything is
twilight, the confusions of evening. Tomaz thinks the world is
moist. He walks on the earth's cliff edge. Darkness hums.
When I read the papers each morning I reinvent geography.
Above me now Jupiter is sliding its way across the sky.
A town in India has sunk twenty feet. The toxic spill in Hungary
is turning its map red again.
                        It is important to keep busy.
Yesterday I went to Ken's grave and put a stone on top of
his stone. In his Paul Jensen story he says you don't have to have
been there to tell it. His characters speak words that are
flooded washes. Like him, what they have is what they give away.
Sometimes everything's for sale. It's as if we were all falling
out of trees. A train crash in the Ukraine, a stoning in Iran,

mud slides in Columbia. You can use one thing to take your mind
off another. Like the head of the policeman in Mexico delivered
in a suitcase. Sometimes I think my corneas are melting.

Now

the dog has sniffed out a few mole holes. They can burrow
a hundred feet a day. Why do dogs appear in so much literature?
When Odysseus returns thinking of revenge, his dog dies.
Actaeon caught a glimpse of Diana and his own dogs ate him.
Tereza's Karenin in *Unbearable Lightness of Being* dies of cancer.
How can Lightness be unbearable when it allows us to do one thing
but think another? All I have to do is drink a little *lemoncello*
and I am right there in Monterroso al Mare with its lemons the size
of grapefruits that Montale wrote about. His poem, *The Storm*, is
really about the coming war which is never mentioned. You can
sense the dead shadows where his lover walked. We can't help
but say one thing and mean another. The way a rock interrupts
the ocean's vision of itself, or the way the mind keeps rearranging
events, like this, to let us think we are more moral than we are.

Where the World Comes to Me

for Earl Braggs

That too, like the possibility of petrified stars, was
a question no one had considered. Or like the forgotten
letter falling from my book. Or the dawn echoing the way
a butterfly opens its wings. Some of the light is
a few billion years old and began in places that no longer
exist. Not to even mention the question of how we got here.
Not the fact of this wheelchair and my torn quadricep,
nor the fact that our DNA relates us to porcupines and
pomegranates. Rather, something in between. I used to be
very indecisive, but now I'm not so sure.

                                          Sometimes
our shadows stick to the ground for years. It's all very
complicated, the way a forensic scientist creates a face
from a fragmented jaw. My own doctor used a weave
that was invented 200 years ago by a French seamstress
to braid tendon, muscle and nerve. It's like the two
ends of the Cancer Constellation whose radiant arms are
intertwined. Or the space elevator that uses a 60,000 mile
cable to link to the space station in the next few decades.

But I was talking about beginnings, and possibility.
I'll add the details you need a little later on. I could
tell you that cornflakes and Graham Crackers began
as remedies for chronic masturbation. That the universe
began as exploding light, followed by bacteria in little
petri dishes of puddles. Bill just sent an email with so many
personal tragedies it makes my own complaints silly.
I should be telling you about all the omissions in this
poem. It's like reading a genuine imitation, and in a random

order. *I was born at a very early age,* said W.C. Fields
for whom everything was a joke.

                         So I should not mention
the family of Emmanuel Aguer, kidnapped in Nairobi
at six years old, who didn't have the $70 ransom to free
him, finding his smashed body later in a sugar sack,
part of a war that seems to have no beginning we can name.
How does anything like that begin? What can we say
that makes any difference? The color of the wind is empty.

From this chair the late shadows look like spears.
Do you think there is an answer for everything?
How does the pileated woodpecker outside my window
know where the insects hide under the bark? Derrida says
all our answers leave traces like the dark spaces where
galaxies have burned out. Stephen Hawking says
all the black holes are leaking. What they leak is time.
The future is already in mothballs. Our hearts are dressed
in rags. The poor moth circling me has been fooled
by this warm autumn. Emmanuel is already gone from
the newspapers. My own name settles behind the hills.
Our words began as symbols, *O* from the Egyptian eye,
E as a man with raised hands, but to what? God? Tomorrow?

The Higgs boson is called the God particle which, if created
in Switzerland, might be the end of the world, or new beginning.
Sometimes I think we are all direction with no place. I wish
I could find an antecedent for all that I've said. Membrane
theory says that every universe we inhabit is made of
the same substance. So maybe there was nothing before us

except ourselves. There's no sense sitting around like
misspelled words.

          A began as the Canaanite figure for an ox.
The stitches on my leg looked like their ancient script found
on cave walls in the Sinai *Valley of Terrors*. Light squints
on the windows. The wind rips at the trees. The first star is
a doorknob. Behind it, an attic of dreams covered in dust,
boxes of forgotten sorrows. Tomorrow I'll begin to clean away
the past. The nightingale will repeat the words we have forgotten.
It's up to you to decide what your question will be. That too.

Prophecy

You exist in the delirious illusion of language.
— *Robert Penn Warren*

What I want to say to you has already disappeared like the flashlight
beam I aimed at empty space years ago. If Augustine was right
it will hit the edge of the universe in 15 billion years. If Einstein was
right then it will never get to the end of it. My own life is orbiting
a word I don't want to land on. Heisenberg said you can only know
where you have been. Freud said that where we are is the terror
of what we were. He was terrified by sex which he saw as a kind
of impalement. Polls say the happiest people are those in the middle
of sex. So tell me, why have you paused to listen?

Most of our words
come with dress codes to hide the world we never want to see.
Some march to the rhythm of goose steps. All I need to do is
throw another stone at the stars to know how far from any center
we are. Even Charon can't say which shore is which.

Every word here tries to pronounce something that has no name.
The words we don't hear are the words that control us. The words
I want to say edge over the horizon like a sunset sail. Every breath
disturbs the next. Every word erases another word. Nathan, the first
prophet, said no one would come after him. So what did he know?

I don't even know what the end of this sentence says because,
while the clock is taking its time to decide, the homeless man
in the cemetery blows a few random notes on a dented trumpet,
a few cigarette butts in the flowerpot have a story they refuse to say,

the wounded day limps home alone, a few more protesters are shot
in Bahrain, a few mothers and children slaughtered in Mexico
in the middle of some drug war.

Isn't everything we say just some
bit of breath we can't hold any longer. Doesn't every word draw
a picture that hides what it really means. How did all those painters
know what the Apocalypse looks like? The bombed church
in Baghdad thought it was today. The man shot on his porch in East
Chattanooga thought it was another day.

Sometimes the moon rises
full of hate. Clouds scramble over distant peaks, the wind broods
in a ravine, the flycatcher, perched alone, waits for darkness.

In truth, what I want to say to you are these trace elements
lingering in the spaces between words. In truth, nothing we say is
worth the way the hawk slides through the invisible air from
the top of the skeleton of a dead tree.

In a few years you'll decipher
how these words will create a whole world I never meant to say.
Our windows have their own prophecies. Birdsong crinkles the air.
Everything we say is a self-portrait. The radio preacher says
that flowers can't bloom in hell. I have it on good report that

you can fit 1,737 angels on the head of a pin, excepting fat angels.
Salvation comes before creation, writes Agamben, which is why
we have to say whatever words, however dark, puddle at the end
of each sentence.

And isn't what we can't say exactly what attracts us?

And you, would it have made any difference if I said what I wanted
to face back at the beginning, that we have to learn to love whatever
truth will say itself, oh, not at the safe distance words create, but
unconditionally, like the woman who cannot understand why she is
impaled on the branch in the Ivory Coast like one of Goya's
Disasters of War discovering words she never knew would lead her there.

Revision

You can smell the sunlight as it stalks us through the weeds
in the abandoned lot. It's like the old dog that circles
before he finds his spot. A few stars defy the town's pink
glow. A few late sounds stagger out from the corner bar.

I'm here because I can't sleep. There's a falcon on the ledge
ready to revise what happens below. Its prey imitates
the backup chirp of the delivery truck approaching
the loading dock.

      I should have begun with that warning sound,
I should have begun when the sun crossed the town of Houla,
Syria, brushing the bodies of the massacred children. They look
like carefully wrapped cocoons.

               Here, time slips down
the side of a building as if it were only a shadow.
Spider webs glisten beneath a fire escape. Someone has
tossed a few broken needles in the gutter. A few bats
scatter the darkness over an alley.
           So, then,
where do you go from there? I can hear but not see
the churning of a river barge. Even the clouds are in a rush
to leave. What you see depends on who you are.

In a little while the TV news comes courtesy of a man's
deodorant. Another gang of illusions announces its sincere
disapproval. Another mass extinction is just waiting for
a new comet.

Why do we so often begin and end with ourselves, with our emotions and their price tags still attached?

Here, there's a single light in a window across the street that shines down on a pigeon caught in a pool of green-blue oil. The town clock refuses to strike. There's a busted shopping cart against the curb. The diseased trees cut down along the avenue are stacked like kindling.

There, troop carriers inject a few militia into the next nightmare.

There was a time when I knew, or seemed to know, how to surrender my shadows to the shadow of the truth. Our memories are like children's pick-up sticks we forget how to grasp.

But in fact, there never was a real beginning. The star whose light approaches is not where it began. You can't trace the origin of the bullets that explore the dreams inside a child's head.

Out of the ruins of these words other ruins arise. They are not going to circle back to be revised.

Someone says the dolphins and pelicans dying off the coast of Peru are also a sign of the end. But there ought to be a better ending than this, better than these few words walking off into the fog, better, certainly, than those boys throwing sticks at a trapped pigeon, but there isn't.

No End to It

Rome

From the outdoor café in the shadow of the old synagogue
I've been watching many shoes complain about the cobblestone.
I've been reading about entanglement which is the way atoms
and cells work together as one. A few dreams levitate
in front of me. The early bats are constantly changing their opinions.
It was from this piazza that the Nazis rounded up thousands
to ship to Bergen-Belsen. A politician seems trapped in his newspaper
photo. People walk on the memories others have left. It was
always a mistake to think the stars will save us.
                              They didn't
save the souls twisted into shadows a few weeks ago from
the tornadoes that stole into towns on the other side of the world.
Trees panicked. Lives landed in gardens miles away with their mail.
The winds had started out indecisive. Soon everyone was clothed
in dogma. The street preacher saying it was our punishment.
His words as broken as our roofs. It was, he screamed, the end
of the world.
            They said that here, too, 1943. History is all
entanglement. The old man at the bus stop across the street
who clutches his watch, the one pushing a cart of all he owns is
remembering the lives he had, his skin splintered, his eyes like
abandoned temples. Everything he felt trails after him like the faint
tail of a comet.
               This is how it becomes entangled with the eddies
of my own memories: with the way your blouse tugged at
the rising wind, with all those shadows I see still searching for
their bodies in this piazza.
                          I can't bear to lose any of it. Not even
the lines I've cut here.

How often our hearts turn into sieves!
They still have not finalized the death figures from the storms.
It is such a small number compared to what happened here.
The word *dark* creates its own night. There are no adjectives
in reality, no numbers that mean anything to anyone whose breath
returns to air.

Our lives roam like imperceptible tidal waves a sailor
notices as a gentle swell too far out at sea to cause concern.
The dead protesters in Syria, the baby suffocated by her father,
there's no end to these entanglements.

Each life becomes like
the piano the storm tossed into the next county that only
the field mice will try to play. There's no telling where we'll find
each other next. There is too much we haven't said, too much
we haven't loved. We leave a few words we hope someone picks up
with our broken branches and our lives—as a kind of fossil evidence.
Science tells us Truth is only the last, most elegant explanation.

So we need history plaques and the stare of a homeless man to remind
us how quickly our dreams are deported as they try desperately
to go on beyond us. At some point we want to know what the ocean
remembers of its rivers, what the crow on the phone wire knows
that allows him to trust the words he sleeps across.

Beyond us
the universe is expanding by exploding its stars, creating what
the astronomers call *entangled nests*, each one with its own
possible ending among an infinite number of possible endings,
as when the man the other day stepped in front of a bus here to give
his dying wife the heart he could not show her when he was alive.

At the Confederate Graveyard, Chattanooga

The world is full of marvelous things that words could not keep.
— Marvin Bell

Starlight blows across the graves of the slaves whose stones
disappeared, or never were. Similarly, the song of some hidden bird
shivers as the light does on the inside of your eyelid. Just as I say
that I realize how easy our words carry us from one thing to another
before we understand what it means.

I think how there are no nouns
in the natural world. And how often it is that what we mean we never
say, but that what we say we often never mean.

Here the leaves seem
to turn into air. The clouds rewrite themselves as other clouds.
All evening I have been haunted to think of you as gone. Across
the path, the stones of Confederate soldiers become their own shadows.
One legend has it that souls wander outside their bodies only
to remember things they never saw. Maybe we are just stories
telling other stories. We think the dead live in us, but it is we who live
in them.

By now that bird is making impossible requests. It seems
to rise out of its own song. Above it, the Milky Way appears as
a huge scythe across the sky which is, I fear, the kind of sign
no one wants to understand. Maybe its stars are just another failure
of darkness. Still, in all that darkness, the Voyager probe is still
looking for the birthmark of the universe. How tragic that we never
speak the one word that gives meaning to what we will become.

Here, moonlight uncovers what is forgotten, but what we remember
stays hidden. It is as if even this mention of you didn't exist.
The horizon crumbles behind a few buildings. How many of those dark
corners of the sky are stars that have burnt out like the names of the lost.

How easy it is for a poem about death to become a poem about love.
How easy it is for our dreams to lie to us. I think that is why the song
of that bird tells us to speak like the wind, because our dreams must
sift through everything if we are to believe what they imagine for us.
I think this is why the Egyptians took out the brain but preserved the heart.
Or why the Brazilian Indians think of people as halves of one another.

What I love are the moments between notes of that marvelous bird.
This is the first thing I have to tell you: inside each of its notes my heart
beats. The empty branches tell us why there is something rather than
nothing.

I know now what the man knew when he called this place
savagely tender. He is sleeping at the far corner where the path ends
as if his story were beyond rescue. But I should tell you also that this
poem has been written over the erased drafts of an earlier poem
whose characters were only these headstones, the way that man
had etched a name above the faded dates of a distant relative.
And this too is a story we live inside when we no longer know
what to call it, a story whose words are the only truth we should
trust, for what is rescued dies, but what is lost lives forever.

Riptide

for my sister, Nancy

How many times have we reduced our lives to a wrinkled map?
How many places has a broken street sign or compass led us?
How many times do we believe the invisible—like the riptide
that ferries the empty skiff into the next state? This morning
everything is so still we can hear the tides turning inside us.
There are vapor trails already shredding the past above us.
An uneasy breeze tears the lazy fog from the sea surface.

What we were is never what we are. A few cormorants
disappear below the swells, then rise to shake off whatever
it is they have dreamt. We are already in heaven, wrote Tillich,
but we have to know where to look. How many times?
We blink almost 20 times a second which gives our brains rest,
according to some scientists, but also means, if you do the math,
we miss seeing for about 730 hours by the time we are fifty
not counting those times we close our eyes hoping to shut
others out.

Near the Black Sea once, I watched three peasants
ride an ox cart down a dirt road towards the edge of the sky.
The light there seemed magnetic, the air seemed to converse
with eternity. I can't explain what that should mean now.
The youngest looked back as if to say these signs were enough
to tell me all I needed to know. The full white spade of the moon
had already started to dig into the earth behind me.

It was
near there that Ovid was exiled among what he called barbarians
who attacked his camp, but also his language for he feared he would

lose his words for love, for fellowship, for self. I think that's why
Kant thought that even God has to ask himself, *Why am I?*
It's a question, given the slaughters in Kenya and Syria,
Pakistan and Iraq, given the faces of the children who look into
the splintered faces of their parents who have been blown
into walls and car fenders, we don't want Him to answer, those
places where we don't want Him to even look.

                          What we see is
what we are. How many times have we wished only to notice
the way the lobster buoys bob just offshore. Or watched graceful
gulls follow the fishermen back to the docks? They seem sometimes
to hover there as if they have stopped time.

                          But forgive me,
for now the sun has climbed above the horizon here without
incident. I remember the way we could trace the invisible
magnetic fields by putting a magnet beneath a sheet of paper
covered with iron filings. It seemed so simple, then, to believe
what we couldn't see. How many times is the world created
when, each morning, we open our eyes? Maybe History is what
we make of it. We live between what exists and what doesn't.

Now the cormorant seems to slide over the surface, content,
a bi-plane is dragging a banner whose message, too, has no special
meaning, except to say we are alive, that we see, when we want,
beyond the curvature of the earth, beyond our own lives,
and into the lives of those children because to see, finally, is
to love the invisible currents that bind us to one another.